What is Stevia?

Benefits, Side Effects, Growing Stevia, Recipes with Stevia

Jeen van der Meer

What is Stevia?

Table of Contents

More Books By
Jeen van der Meer

Is Coffee Good For You? Discover the powerful health benefits of coffee

To see all my books go to
Amazon.com: Jeen van der Meer: Books

What is in stevia

Stevia comes from the family of sunflower plants. It grows naturally in the tropical regions of South American and in some of the subtropical regions of the western part of North America. The scientific name for stevia is *Stevia rebaudiana*.

It goes by other names like *sugarleaf, sweetleaf* or *sweet leaf.* Many just call it stevia, for short.

Stevia is a very strong sugar substitute, meaning if you use too much it goes beyond sweet to bitter with a bitter after taste if too much is used. People grow stevia for the sweetness contained in the leaves.

Stevia is **300 times sweeter than cane sugar**. Stevia is **a lot healthier** than cane sugar because it does not turn into fat in the body once consumed. Stevia is a great sugar substitute for people who are on a **diet to lose fat** and for **diabetics**.

Because stevia is not a carbohydrate, it is the perfect sugar substitute for those on **low-carbohydrate diets**. Stevia does not raise or lower the blood glucose. It is the perfect sweetener for those on low glycemic diets, or a **diabetic diet**. Stevia in small amounts gives a nice sweet flavor in foods, and does not add fat to the body.

How to grow stevia

Stevia plants grow naturally in the tropical regions of South America, but you do not need to move south in order to grow these. Stevia may be an exotic plant, but it adapts well in North America even as far north as southern Canada.

Commercially grown stevia is more concentrated than that of home grown. Commercial **stevia extract** (the white powder) has a concentration of over **90 % of stevioside** as compared to home grown which yields around 12%.

What this means is you may need more home grown to achieve the level of sweetness you desire, or use homegrown to supplement commercial stevia (which can be quite pricey).

Insect repellant

The good news about growing stevia is the ability for the plants to naturally repel insects. This makes it easier as you do not have to worry about bugs eating the plants before you can harvest them. It may be also smart to plant stevia around in a garden to help repel pesky insects from other plants as well. Even the grasshoppers will avoid them. You will not find an aphid or locust anywhere near these sweet leaves. This helps them to be maintenance free as far as having to deal with insecticide. This is good in the tropical and sub tropical areas where insects are normally a big issue, like Florida.

Growing the plants

Stevia plants can be grown from a plot of ground in your back yard, or from a container on your deck or patio. It is legal to grow Stevia, and easy enough that you can produce nice plants right from planters or in sections in the yard or garden.

That said, getting the plants to actually grow is another issue. It is very difficult to take stevia seeds and produce a plant worthy of being useful as a sweetener. Many of the plants grown this way are too weak to use and rendered useless. You want a plant with strong stevioside levels, so it will yield the results you desire.

To grow a successful garden with stevia is to start with seedlings and stevia plants that have already started to grow. You can find such seedlings at a nursery or at a store that sells herbalist supplies. It may not be that easy, you may have to call around in order to find these, but they are well worth the search. If you cannot find these plants locally, you can find websites online that will ship the seedlings to you. You will want to start with seedlings that can produce plants high in stevioside, so be sure to inquire about that. **The higher the concentration of stevioside, the sweeter the leaves** are, and this is what you are after.

Stevia plants do well in **steady temperatures** of around 60 degrees Fahrenheit (around 16° Celsius) or higher. You cannot successfully plant stevia in cold soil because it will die.

The plants do well if set about **two feet (60 cm) apart** all the way around. They grow tall to almost three feet (1 meter), and spread out a good two feet in width. They need **plenty of room** and days that do not reach freezing temperatures. **Do not plant** them if the nights **drop below 50 degrees** Fahrenheit (10° C).

Stevia plants thrive in **soil that is rich and fertile**. They do well in potting soil that has fertilizer and plant food mixed in already.

The **root** system grows **parallel to the ground** rather than deep. Planting the seedlings in fertile soil helps to start a plant, **add good compost** along the parameter of the plant to continue feeding the root system. Stevia does not need an excessive amount of water. **Over watering** the plants will cause **stunted growth**. Make sure the garden area drains well and does not stand in water or is prone to flooding.

Looking after Stevia plants

Water the plants if necessary to **keep the soil from completely drying out**, careful to not over water. The compost on top of the root area will help the soil to drain and will help to hold the right amount of moisture on the roots.

Fertilize the plants to keep them growing healthy. Using an organic fertilizer works well, especially one that is low in nitrogen. Too much nitrogen is not good for the plants. Organic fertilizers tend to keep the nitrogen levels low enough they will not harm stevia plants.

Stevia plants need to be **harvested** well **before** the **first frost**, but the weather needs to be on the cool side in order to give the best leaves. Once the plant is fully grown, it can withstand cooler temperatures.

It is during the early growth stages that cooler temperatures are more harmful. The longer a stevia plant can grow in shorter cooler days, the sweeter the leaves will become.

If a frost happens early, before the leaves are ready for harvesting, **cover them during the freezing temperatures** to give the plants more time to produce sweeter leaves. By doing this you can add another couple of weeks growth.

Harvesting

Use pruning shears to start the harvest of the stevia. Gingerly cut the branches first, prior to stripping out the leaves. Leaves contain the most sweetness you are after, but if you take care in clipping the stems of the leaves, you will garner a bit more of the sweetness, to make the stevia stretch even further.

Your goal is to harvest the part of the plant that has the **most stevioside**, which are the **leaves** and the **stems**. Everything else can go. It is easier to strip the stems and leaves, if you have the branches in your hands rather than trying to cut the stems and leaves right from the plant with the branches intact.

For people who live in more tropical weather, like Florida, the stevia plants are able to live through the winter okay. Proper pruning will help the plant to survive through the winter.

When harvesting the branches, make sure to **leave around four inches** (approx 10 cm) of branch from the base. If you do this, the branch will grow back out the following spring, giving you a second crop of stevia stems and leaves.

Two years is about the maximum time of life for a stevia plant. Rarely will you be able to have a rich harvest from a plant that is three years or older, after the second year, replant with new seedlings.

If you live in a climate that has frost and freezing winters the stevia plants will not survive. Cuttings will help to create the new crop next spring. Take as many cuttings as you need for the new crop next spring.

Cuttings survive well by allowing them to root first. You can use a solution made from willow tree tips (which pulverized) or a solution created from rooting hormones commercially.

Soak the cuttings in the solution, then plant in a root medium for around three weeks, allowing plenty of time for the roots to form. You can then pot the seedlings in small pots (under six inches (15cm) is fine) and kept inside in a sunny spot through the winter, to wait planting the next spring.

What to do with the harvest

After you harvest the **leaves and stems**, they **need to be dried**. Lay them out over a net or a screen, something that will allow good airflow around them. Heat is not required to dry the leaves, but good airflow helps the process along. Laying the leaves on a surface that allows for airflow from underneath.

If the temperatures are above freezing, you can place the leaves and stems in the sun for half a day and they will completely dry. The key to a successful crop is to **dry them as fast as possible**. Drying longer than 12 hours will cause the stevioside to be less. A food dehydrator is useful, however for best results, dry for 12 hours in the sun.

Once the leaves are dry, you may crush them to create the sweetener. Crushing the leaves is rather easy, hand crush works well, or use a coffee grinder or herb blender.

Crush into a fine powder. Create liquid stevia by blending 1/4 cup of crushed leaves and stems with 1 cup of warm water. Allow to sit at room temperature overnight for up to 24 hours, then store in the refrigerator.

This is a good method if you have room to store the liquid. If refrigerator storage is a problem, store the crushed leaves and stems in an airtight container in your cupboard.

Growing stevia in containers

If you do not have a garden spot for your stevia plants, you can grow them in containers on your balcony or deck. This is good news for people who live in apartments or have tiny yards and want to grow stevia.

A good container needs to be around a foot (30 cm) in diameter and fill the container with a good potting soil or growing mix. Add mulch or compost on top to help nourish the almost to the surface roots.

Keep the containers in the sun for best result. Treat the plants the same as above. If you live in a frost zone, you can bring the containers in during the winter, after pruning to get two years of harvest from the plants.

Benefits of stevia

Stevia is fast becoming a favored sugar-substitute among those who love to eat organic and natural foods. Unlike other artificial sweeteners, **stevia is 100% natural**, with no harmful chemicals. You never hear of people having bad reactions to stevia like you do for aspartame or sucralose.

A while back it was almost impossible to find stevia in regular grocery stores, but now that it has some of the spotlight as a great sugar alternative, grocery stores are starting to stock it on their shelves. You can find stevia by itself or in a combined mixture with other sugar substitutes.

Stevia is 300 times sweeter than sugar

Because stevia is around 300 times sweeter than cane sugar, you need to use much less to sweeten foods. The Japanese developed a refining process that pulls the sweet ingredient, stevioside, from the leaves and stems.

In Japan, stevia is a very popular choice as a sugar substitute. The commercial sweetener industry there sells almost 50% of the sugar substitute as stevia. The FDA in the United States had made it impossible to sell stevia as a sugar substitute for several years until finally in 1995 they allowed it to be sold if the label stated it was a dietary supplement. This kept the industry from promoting stevia as a sugar substitute for years, until now; people are discovering this well kept secret.

No Calories

The main benefit of stevia is the ability to be a sweetener without the harmful effects of actual sugar. Stevia has zero calories and yet is much sweeter than cane sugar. The best stevia grows in regions of South America and Mexico due to the tropical climates.

The poorest quality stevia comes from China, which produces plants that are not as sweet, again, due to the climate. You can quickly tell the difference from stevia imported from China over those imported from Mexico and South America. It pays to find out where the stevia comes from and make sure to purchase the ones that will be sweeter to the taste.

Liquid Stevia

It is easier to find liquid stevia, since more companies are making the solution. The **best liquid stevia is water based**, which is a lot better than an alcohol-based solution. The concentration of the stevioside stays higher in water-based solutions.

Stevia has qualities other than as a sweetener. Stevia **helps with skin and scalp conditions**. If stevia is in an alcohol-based solution, the medicinal qualities become diluted and ineffective. Water based solutions keep the stevioside pure and strong. The higher the concentration of stevia leaves and stems to the water, the better quality the final product is.

Those sweet leaves

The sweetness of stevia stays in the leaves and stems. High concentrations can leave a bitter taste or a licorice taste in the mouth. By creating a liquid stevia, enough is diluted to make the bitterness go away.

The bitter flavor specifically comes from the leaf veins. It is wise to remove these veins (or as many as possible) during processing so the bitterness will go away. The sweetness is in the meat of the leaf and the stem, the more leaf present, the less leaf veins, the sweeter the flavor. The more leaf veins present, the more likely is that the sweetness will have a bitter after taste.

Sweet without regrets

Stevia benefits diabetics because it helps to regulate the body's blood sugar. Diabetics have trouble regulating sugar; the levels can go too high or too low, especially if a diabetic consumes cane sugar.

Consuming stevia is beneficial because it aids in the regulation of the blood sugars levels. Stevia also helps to **regulate blood pressure**, if a person has hypertension; consuming stevia seems to help it stay at a lower normal level. South America sells stevia for the sole purpose of helping people with diabetes, low blood sugar, and hypertension.

Fighting infections

Liquid stevia has further benefits beyond what it does for health. Liquid stevia holds up well by inhibiting the growth of bacteria that can invade food products. Because of these properties, stevia works well in preventing harmful bacteria from forming on teeth and gums.

Harmful bacteria on the teeth causes tooth decay, so **stevia helps to prevent tooth decay**. Many create a mouthwash out of stevia by placing a few drops of the liquid stevia in about 1/4 cup of water and then gargle and rinse through the mouth. It is safe to swallow, unlike many commercial mouthwashes. People doing this on a regular basis also report a lower incident of viruses such as the common cold and influenza.

Skin Care with Stevia

A further benefits of stevia is to help with certain skin problems. Liquid stevia made from water helps to heal skin ailments of acne, eczema, and seborrhea dermatitis.

Liquid stevia has **healing properties** to help wounds and helps to minimize scarring. It stings when applied, but the pain is quickly numbed. Some physicians use liquid stevia to treat **psoriasis, cancer, and cold sores** on the mouth. There is no argument that the healing properties of stevia exist and work well. Next time you have a cut or sore, try a dab and see for yourself how well it heals.

The healing properties of stevia come from stevia liquid made from adding water to crushed leaves and stems. The processed stevioside like Japan manufacturers makes the best sweetener, but not the best on skin (it does not have the healing properties like the homemade liquid stevia).

However, stevioside is highly recommended for diabetics and anyone with blood sugar issues because it helps to regulate and normalize blood sugars. Stevioside sweetener has no calories and is much sweeter than cane sugar or other artificial sweeteners with no side effects.

Save all around

Stevia is completely safe, many scientist and physicians have studied and researched its qualities and have found no evidence of bad side effects. In all the trials run to date, there are no contradicting results when tested both dietary and on the skin.

The observation of the cells and membrane characteristics found absolutely no changes from consumption or application of stevia. When tested on lab animals, they emerged without cancers and they are birth defect free. They discovered no fluctuations in food intake or anything negative to the human body.

Stevia Side Effects

All this talk about the benefits of stevia and some may still wonder if there are any side effects at all. The truth is, after all the research and testing, they have found no ill side effects with humans. The United States and Europe refused to allow it to be sold as a food due to the lack of research and studies in these particular studies.

Most of the studies occurred in South America, Mexico and Japan. Recently, **Europe lifted the ban** on selling stevia as a food additive and now they offer it for use in beverages and food.

Some experiments gave rats a high dosage of stevia, which later showed a toxic response in the male rats. These experiments did not show a striking negative result, but enough to raise concern. However, they did not perform the experiments using the correct protocol for such studies, which rendered the results as inconclusive.

The experiment gave the male rats such a high dose of steviol (the substance in stevia that people question) that if a human tried to consume that much it would taste horrible. The equivalent of the steviol given to the rats would equal to a man eating half his weight in steviol, which would essentially be impossible.

Not only did the experiment give the high dosage of steviol, it would have to be that a human would have to consume that much on a daily basis. You can clearly see why this experiment is useless. If you drank half your body weight in plain water daily, that would become toxic too.

If a human replaces stevia with their sugar intake that equals to around four grams of crushed stevia leaves. Not quite what would be equal to the 75 to 100 pounds if you go with the amount the rats took in during the experiment?

Stevia has been around for hundreds of years, used by many cultures. The past thirty years shows that stevia sweetens foods in Brazil and Japan with no problems. In the United States stevia is used as a food additive since as recently as 2008, where stevia is an ingredient in a sugar substitute.

After all the research, experiments, and studies, there are no conclusive findings, that stevia is anything but a **very good substance to use as a sweetener** and as a **remedy for skin ailments**. If there had been bad side effects in humans, there would be records from Japan and Brazil and there are not any.

Stevia and Weight Loss

Using stevia as a sweetener helps to facilitate fat burning and weight loss. Ask the women of Asia who enjoy their desserts created with stevia while losing weight rapidly. They will tell you stevia is a perfect replacement of the high caloric sugar, and that it sweetens their desserts so well they do not even miss sugar.

Stevia is a lot safer than artificial sweeteners which have a long list of ill side effects, including allergies that could be life threatening. Just ask someone who has a verified allergy to Aspartame, they will tell you how scary it is to ingest the stuff. Stevia is a wonderful alternative because it is completely and one hundred percent natural.

Manufacturers are beginning to see the virtues in using stevia to sweeten their food products. It may be a slow turn around, but you can pick up foods now and see stevia on the ingredient list. As stevia becomes more accepted, you will find it sweetening more foods.

Start requesting it in stores, contact manufacturers, and ask them to sweeten their foods with stevia instead of those artificial sweeteners. If enough people speak up, they will listen. Right now, heath food stores carry most stevia and stevia products.

For successful fat burning and weight loss, you need to do a change of lifestyle. You need to eat right, cut out all sugared foods and processed junk foods, and eat healthy. Eating healthy includes fresh fruits and vegetables, lean meats.

The good thing about sweetening with stevia is you can continue to enjoy your desserts, as long as stevia is the sweetener and not cane sugar. **Stevia can sweeten** anything sugar does, including **beverages**, **cereals**, **cakes**, **cookies, candies** and any type of **dessert**. The only difference in cooking with stevia is you use a lot less compared to sugar.

Stevia and exercise is the way to go

Stevia helps with weight loss for the simple fact that it helps to keep the sweet cravings away (because you can sweeten your food with it, therefore you will not be tempted to eat those high calorie desserts.)

In addition, the fact that stevia helps to regulate blood sugar, so you feel better, not sluggish. If you add exercise to the plan, **the weight will melt off**, as long as you stick with it. Change your eating habits and weight will not be an issue for too long. Keep up with the changes so you will keep the weight off permanently.

It is important to avoid certain foods or certain ingredients at all costs when you are dieting. Of course, sugar and high fructose corn syrup are bad; they turn to fat in the body. However, avoid artificial sweeteners too which can have adverse affects.

Aspartame causes the body to slow down on fat burning. While aspartame itself is non-caloric, it does not aid the body in weight loss. You want to stay away from the other artificial sweeteners too.

Anything that is not natural can cause issues and have adverse affects. **Stevia is 100% natural**, so stick with stevia for the best way to sweeten foods naturally without calories.

Have you tried other fad diets and failed?

Is it hard to keep up with what you are suppose to eat, counting calories, counting fat, eat this, not that. It is too much. We have complicated dieting to the point that people give up before they start.

Dieting or proper nutrition is simple really. Stick with eating fresh whole foods, foods that grew in the earth, fruits, and vegetables. Eat lean meats. Stay away from processed foods, fast foods, convenient foods. Sweeten with stevia. Exercise at least three times a week, and drink plenty of water. That diet cannot fail if you stick with it.

Stevia and Diabetes

Diabetes is the body's inability to process insulin, which helps the body to deal with glucose. When this is off, eating too much sugar can be deadly. A diabetic has to check his blood sugar often, normally several times a day.

Diabetics choose from the array of artificial sweeteners to sweeten their foods, but are these nutritious? Most "diet" foods contain artificial sweeteners like aspartame and sucralose these days. People on diets reach for these items, but diabetics have to, they have little choice.

The bad thing about artificial sweeteners is the manmade chemicals, which can be harmful. **Many people have an allergy to aspartame**, which **causes migraine headaches** and eventually seizures if they do not cease consumption of them.

What is a diabetic to do if they develop sensitivity to these artificial sweeteners? Eat foods that are bitter and bland? Now that stevia is more available, they have a viable option, a safe option that not only sweetens their food but also is also beneficial.

More physicians are suggesting the switch to the all-natural stevia over all the other artificial sweeteners.

Completely Natural

There are **no bad artificial chemicals** or ingredients in stevia. By itself it is one hundred percent all natural with no side effects. Stevia is almost **three hundred times sweeter** than cane sugar, so you only use just a tiny bit to sweeten foods.

Stevia is much sweeter tasting than the other artificial sweeteners too. Stevia may appear to cost more than other sweeteners, but because you use so much less you actually are not spending any more on stevia than you are on cane sugar or any other artificial sweetener. Because you use less stevia to sweeten, a little goes a long way.

Better than artificial sweeteners

Stevia has zero calories, and it will not raise blood sugar in a diabetic. It has a zero on the glycemic index too. Stevia offers a natural alternative to artificial sweeteners and a healthier alternative to cane sugar.

Stevia does not turn into glucose in the body, **nor does it turn into fat**. It is the best zero calorie low carb solution for a sweetener for diabetics. Any food that uses cane sugar as a sweetener can use stevia as a sweetener.

Stevia has benefits, which includes helping the body to regular blood sugar, which helps a normal insulin release. **Stevia helps diabetics** to manage their blood sugars better. In addition, stevia helps people suffering from hypoglycemia and hyperglycemia due to the ability to regulate blood sugars.

Physicians in South America use stevia to treat diabetes regularly, because they realize stevia has properties that help the body to manage blood sugar. They have found stevia helps people with hypertension too. Stevia works to tone the heart muscle.

It is therefore, recommended if you are diabetic to **check with your physician before starting on stevia**. If they do not know about it, ask them to research it, as it has such good benefits in treating both diabetes and hypertension.

Because stevia is an herb, it is advisable to seek the advice of your healthcare provider always before using such a product if you suffer from any blood sugar disorder.

Stevia does not affect blood sugar, does not increase it. Stevia allows diabetics to be able to sweeten foods that they otherwise cannot eat. The marketplace is full of stevia recipe books.

Stevia goes well in recipes as a sugar replacement in China, Japan, Mexico, and South America for years. Stevia recipes include cookies, cakes, pies, and other equally sweet desserts.

Now a diabetic can create dishes that originally called for sugar and substitute stevia to maintain the delicious sweet flavor. Use stevia while cooking wherever sugar is called for, only be sure to read the instructions first.

Where to Buy Stevia

Stevia is becoming more available on the shelves of regular grocery stores now. Health food stores carry both liquid and powdered stevia. The internet has many websites selling heath food and websites that sell organic and natural foods including stevia in all forms. Ask your favorite stores if they will stock stevia for you if they do not offer it yet.

You can find stevia on Amazon by searching for: Stevia products

Stevia Powder

If you compare a teaspoon of stevia powder to a teaspoon of sugar - that one little teaspoon is up to three hundred times sweeter. By using this analogy, you can see how little you need to sweeten something that calls for a "teaspoon of sugar," just a smidgen really.

Stevia is very sweet, and if you have used sugar all your life and switch to stevia, it can take a little bit to get use to the sweeter flavor and the need to reduce greatly the amount used. If you are used to using an artificial sweetener, you will find that stevia powder is so much better, mainly because it is all **natural with no ill side effects**.

Stevia powder is the almost perfect food for everyone.

Anyone who wants to lose weight.
Anyone who wants to prevent cavities.
Anyone who wants to avoid an unhealthy rise in their blood sugar.

Stevia is a perfect sweetener that will sweeten the foods without giving you a "sugar high and then a sugar crash." In addition, unlike sugar, which can egg on a yeast infection, stevia does not affect or encourage the growth of yeast in the body. For people who suffer from an overgrowth of yeast, especially yeast that grows out of hand in the intestinal tracks, stevia will not aggravate the condition.

Stevia powder is one of the safest sweeteners on the market today. Stevia is a plant, an herb, and the powder comes from crushing the leaves and stems. Stevia comes from the Chrysanthemum family. It is in the same family as chamomile and tarragon (which are harmless herbs).

It is related to artichokes, lettuce, safflower oil, and sunflowers. The South American Indians have used stevia for literally hundreds of years because stevia grows wild there. This is why today stevia is widely available there as a sweetener.

Stevia powder comes in a white powder as well as a rough green powder and the brownish liquid known as liquid stevia. Many recipe books call for the white powder, because it most closely resembles sugar.

People associate the white powder to the white powder of sugar. Sometimes the stevia powder is hard to measure just right. There is a way to create liquid stevia out of the powder, and many recipes call for this for a more accurate measurement.

Normally a mixture of three tablespoons to one teaspoon of stevia powder makes a good liquid stevia concentration. Always use filtered water for best results and refrigerate.

If you use more than the tiniest pinch of powdered stevia you will find it is excessively sweet. Because it takes so little powder to sweeten a cup of coffee, or a bowl of cereal, it is very difficult to control.

If you cannot get a hold of the liquid stevia, make it as described above so you can have better control. One tiny drop will likely sweeten it as would a whole teaspoon of cane sugar.

Baking with Stevia - Sweet Yam Pie

Love those sweet potato pies? This is a pie made with yams and sweetened with stevia, for a delicious lower calorie twist on a favorite.

Prep: Preheat oven to 400 degrees Fahrenheit (200° C) and bake the 4 yams for an hour on a baking sheet, until soft and pulpy. Allow to cool and reduce oven temperature to 350 degrees Fahrenheit (175°C). Spray a 9-inch (22 cm) pie plate with non-stick spray.

Pie Crust Ingredients:

2 cups of almond flour (blanched)
1/3 cup of oil (almond or coconut) OR butter
2 teaspoons of vanilla
1/4 teaspoon of baking soda
1/4 teaspoon of liquid stevia
pinch of salt

Mix the almond flour, baking soda, and salt. Slowly add in the oil or butter, vanilla and liquid stevia until well mixed. Pat dough into the pie pan, pressing to make it even. Bake for 10 minutes and allow cooling completely before filling.

Filling Ingredients:

4 yams (garnets)
1 orange (juice and zest only)
2/3 cup of tofu (firm)

1 teaspoon of liquid stevia
1/2 teaspoon of cinnamon
1/2 teaspoon of ginger
1/4 teaspoon of cloves

Peel and mash the yams together with the tofu in a food processor. Slowly add in the orange juice, zest, stevia, cinnamon, ginger, and cloves and process together until mixture is nice and smooth, taking time to scrape the sides. Pour filling into the baked pie crust and bake at 350 degrees Fahrenheit for half an hour. Cool enough to handle pie. Delicious served either warm or cool.

Baking with Stevia - Pecan Maple Pie

Prep: Preheat oven to 350 degrees Fahrenheit (175°C).
Spray a 9-inch (22 cm) pie pan with non-stick spray.

Ingredients for pie crust:

1 1/3 cups of flour (all purpose)
1/3 cup of butter
4 tablespoons of water

Cut the ingredients together in a bowl to form soft dough.
Line the pan, pressing the dough to make it even.
Refrigerate.

Ingredients for filling:

1 1/2 cups of pecan halves (roasted)
1 cup of maple syrup (sugar free)
1/4 cup of butter
3 eggs
2 teaspoons of flour (all purpose)
1 teaspoon of vanilla
1/2 teaspoon of white stevia powder

Mix the stevia powder into the maple syrup to create the sweetened syrup. In pan over low heat, bring the maple syrup stevia mixture to a boil but do not stir. When mixture first begins to boil, turn heat off and remove pan from heat. Mix in the butter, which will melt. Add in the flour and vanilla. Beat the eggs separately, and then slowly stir in the mixture. Spread the pecans on the pie crust, pour the filling over the pecans, they will float to the top. Bake for 40 minutes, cool before serving.

Baking with Stevia - Banana Nut Bread

Prep: Preheat oven to 350 degrees Fahrenheit (175°C). Grease a 7.5 x 3.5 x 2.5 loaf pan.

Ingredients:

2 ripe large bananas
2 cups of flour (whole wheat pastry)
1/2 of buttermilk or plain yogurt
1/2 cup of walnuts (chopped)
1/3 cup of oil (vegetable or canola)
1 egg
1 tablespoon of lemon juice
1 teaspoon of vanilla
1/2 teaspoon of liquid stevia
1/2 teaspoon of baking soda
1/4 teaspoon of white stevia powder
1/4 teaspoon of salt

In a small bowl mash the bananas and then mix in the liquid and powdered stevia with the lemon juice. In a separate bowl, mix the flour, baking soda, and salt. In a third bowl, beat the oil and egg together to a creamy mixture. Mix in the buttermilk or yogurt and vanilla. Add the banana mixture, blend well. Gently stir in the flour mixture, not over-stirring. Mix in the walnuts, stir until just mixed. Pour mixture into the greased loaf pan and bake up to one hour or until inserted toothpick comes out clean. Pop out of pan and allow cooling before serving.

Cookies with Stevia - Almond Cookies

Prep: Preheat oven to 325 degrees Fahrenheit(160°C). Line a cookie sheet with parchment sheets.

Ingredients:

1 cup of almond flour
1/4 cup of coconut oil
1/4 cup of coconut flakes
30 drops of liquid stevia
2 tablespoons of almond butter (made from raw almonds)
2 teaspoons of almond extract
1/4 teaspoon of salt

Mix together all the ingredients until the mixture forms a soft dough. Drop by the tablespoons onto the parchment covered cookie sheet. Bake for up to an hour and a half until golden brown. Cool completely. Store the uneaten cookies in the refrigerator.

Cookies with Stevia - Chocolate Chip Cookies

Prep: Preheat oven to 350 degrees Fahrenheit(175°C). and lightly spray a cookie sheet with non-stick spray.

Ingredients:

2 cups of flour (all purpose)
1 1/4 cup of chocolate chips
1 cup of butter
1 egg
1 teaspoon of vanilla
3/4 teaspoon of salt
3/4 teaspoon of baking powder
1/2 teaspoon of white stevia powder

Mix the flour, baking powder, and salt and put to the side. In a separate bowl mix the egg, vanilla and stevia powder with an electric mixer. Mix in the butter, mixing until batter is creamy. Slowly add the flour mixture, stirring with a spoon. Gently stir in the chocolate chips. Drop by rounded teaspoons onto the cookie sheet and allow two inches between cookies. Bake for around 25 minutes or until golden brown.

Cookies with Stevia - Shortbread Cookies

Prep: Preheat oven to 350 degrees Fahrenheit(175°C).. Line a cookie sheet with parchment paper.

Ingredients:

1 cup of flour (whole wheat)
1/2 cup of butter
1/2 cup of rice flour (brown)
6 packets of stevia

Mix the flour with the packets of stevia. To the dry ingredients, add in the butter to form a soft dough. You may use your hands. Pull off to form small balls then press the balls into the size of cookies you want on the parchment lined cookie sheet. Bake for 10 minutes, do not allow to brown. Carefully remove and cool on a cookie rack. Shortbread cookies are fragile, do not stack.

Cookies with Stevia - Raisin Oatmeal Cookies

Prep: Preheat oven to 375 degrees Fahrenheit(190°C) and grease a cookie sheet.

Ingredients:

1 1/2 cups of rolled oats
1 cup of flour (whole wheat pastry)
1/2 cup of packed raisins
1/2 cup of butter
5 ounces of apple juice
1/3 cup of walnuts or cashews (ground)
1/4 cup of flour (soy)
1/4 cup of milk
1 egg
1 teaspoon of vanilla
1 teaspoon of baking soda
1 teaspoon of cinnamon
3/4 teaspoon of liquid stevia
1/2 teaspoon of maple flavoring
1/4 teaspoon of salt

Simmer in a small pan the apple juice and raisins for around 15 minutes. Mix the butter, nuts, and soy flour in a bowl. Beat the egg and stir into the butter mixture along with the vanilla, maple flavoring, and stevia. Take 1/3 of the apple juice/raisin mixture and blend in a blender until creamy. Set the remaining apple juice and raisins aside. Add the creamy apple juice/raisin to the butter batter. Slowly stir in the oats and milk. In a separate bowl, mix the pastry flour, baking soda, cinnamon with the salt. Slowly add the dry ingredients to the batter, careful not to over mix. Add in the remaining apple juice and raisins, gently folding into the batter.

Drop by spoonfuls on the greased cookie sheet; flatten with the back of the spoon or the palm of your hand. Bake for around 14 minutes, cool before serving.

Stevia Cake Recipes – Chestnut Cake

Prep: Preheat oven to 450 degrees Fahrenheit(230°C). Oil the bottom of an 11-inch baking pan with 2 tablespoons of oil (canola or olive).

Ingredients:

3 cups of flour (chestnut)
2 1/2 cups of water
1/3 cup of raisins
1/4 cup of pine nuts
4 tablespoons of oil (olive or canola)
1/4 teaspoon of white stevia powder
pinch of salt

Place the water and raisins in a pan and heat on medium heat, until the raisins re-plump and turn soft. Once the raisins are soft, separate the water from the raisins. In a separate bowl, mix together the flour, the separated raisin water, 2 tablespoons of olive or canola oil, salt and stevia, until a soft dough forms. Add in the remaining raisins and nuts and blend well. Pour the batter into the 11 inch oiled baking pan. Sprinkle the remaining 2 tablespoons of oil over the top and bake for around 20 minutes. Cake it done when the top starts to crack. Remove from oven and drain the oil, and then remove from pan for cooling. This is also a gluten free cake.

Stevia Cake Recipes - Ginger Chocolate Cake

Prep: Preheat oven to 350 degrees Fahrenheit(175°C) and grease an 8-inch baking dish.

Ingredients:

1 cup of flour (whole wheat pastry)
1 cup of milk
1/4 cup of cocoa (unsweetened)
1/4 cup of ginger (crystallized and chopped)
1/4 cup of applesauce
35 drops of liquid stevia
2 tablespoons of coconut oil
1 teaspoon of vanilla
1 teaspoon of baking powder
1/2 teaspoon of salt

In a large bowl, mix the applesauce, milk, stevia, coconut oil, and vanilla. In a separate bowl, mix the dry ingredients of flour, cocoa, baking powder, and salt. Slowly combine the dry ingredients into the applesauce mixture. Gently fold in the ginger. Pour batter into the greased baking dish and bake for around 20 minutes or until inserted toothpick comes out clean. Cool before serving.

Stevia Cake Recipes - Carrot Cake

Prep: Preheat oven to 350 degrees Fahrenheit. Oil a 6 inch x10 inch baking pan.

Ingredients:

2 cups of carrots (grated)
1 cup of flour (whole wheat pastry)
1 cup of flour (white unbleached)
8 ounce can of crushed pineapple (with juice)
1/2 cup of coconut flakes (unsweetened)
1/2 cup of butter
1/2 cup of walnuts (chopped)
1/3 cup of yogurt (plain)
1/4 cup of milk
2 eggs (room temperature and slightly beaten)
3 tablespoons of sugar (date)
2 tablespoons of flour (soy)
2 teaspoons of baking powder
1 1/2 teaspoons of cinnamon
1 teaspoon of powdered stevia
1 teaspoon of vanilla
1 teaspoon of baking soda
1/2 teaspoon of maple flavoring
1/2 teaspoon of salt

Combine all but 2 ounces of the pineapple and juice with the coconut and let soak. In a large bowl, mix the butter until creamy, add in the stevia, and date sugar. Slowly mix in the eggs. Then mix the yogurt and milk together and pour into the batter. Stir in the vanilla and maple flavoring. Fold in the walnuts along with the pineapple and coconut mixture, last stir in the grated carrots. In a separate bowl, mix the dry ingredients of the flours, baking powder, baking soda, cinnamon, and salt. Slowly add the dry ingredients into the batter, and stir until blended, not over-mixing. This is a thick batter. Slowly pour the thick batter into the pan and bake for 60 minutes. Leave in pan to cool and frost with cream cheese frosting.

Ingredients for cream cheese frosting:

8 ounces of cream cheese (softened)
1/2 lemon rind (finely grated)
2 tablespoons of milk
1 1/2 tablespoon of lemon juice
1 tablespoon of honey
1/2 teaspoon of white stevia powder

Cream the cream cheese and milk together. Mix in lemon juice and rind with the stevia and honey. Whip together until spreadable and spread over cake.

Ice Cream with Stevia - Lemon Ice Cream

Ingredients:

2 cups of heavy whipping cream
1 cup of milk
1/2 cup of lemon juice
2 tablespoons of lemon peel (fresh grated)
1/2 teaspoon of white stevia powder

Whisk together the milk and stevia, dissolving the stevia completely. Whisk in the whipping cream, lemon juice and lemon peel, until well mixed. Immediately pour mixture into an ice cream maker and mix for half an hour. Store in freezer

Ice Cream with Stevia - Cookie Dough Ice Cream

Ingredients:

4 cups of heavy cream
2 cups of milk
2 cups of light cream
1 cup of chocolate chip cookie dough
   (can use   refrigerator cookie dough, or cookie dough
      made from stevia)
1 tablespoon of vanilla
1 3/4 teaspoon of white stevia powder
1/2 teaspoon of salt

Pour the milk in a pan and on medium high heat allow the milk to scald (bubbles around the edge). Take from heat and mix in the stevia and salt, stirring until dissolved. Gently mix in the creams and vanilla. Cover tightly and set in the refrigerator for half an hour. Pour mixture into your ice cream maker, making the ice cream as the manufacturer suggests in the instructions. Chill, and then stir in the chocolate chip cookie dough. Serve..

Ice Cream with Stevia - Strawberry Ice Cream

Ingredients:

3 cups of strawberries - tops removed
2 cups of half and half cream
1 cup of heavy whipping cream
2 eggs
1 1/4 teaspoon of white stevia powder
1/4 teaspoon of vanilla

Mix in a food processor the strawberries, to a puree mixture. Whip the eggs in a separate bowl, mix in the creams, stevia, and vanilla. Fold in the pureed strawberries. Pour the mixture into an ice cream maker and follow manufacturer's instructions. Continue to freeze in freezer for 4 hours

More Information

I hope you have enjoyed my book, giving you an insight into what stevia is and how you can use it.

In my opinion the future belongs to stevia. Stevia has so many advantages over ordinary sugar without the disadvantages like obesity, tooth decay, diabetes.

Sweet and healthy don't have to be opposites with the help of stevia.

You might also be interested in this book by
Lynda Warwick:

Your Sugar Smart Diet -
The Fast Way To Weight Loss and Health

66097091R00030